THE BEST WAY TO GET YOUR WAY

Written by Tanya Lloyd Kyi

Illustrated by Chanelle Nibbelink

KIDS CAN PRESS

ACKNOWLEDGMENTS

Many thanks to Kathleen Keenan, Amy Tompkins, Barb Kelly,
Genie MacLeod, Margaret Allen and Doeun Rivendell
for bringing this book to life.

Published in Canada and the U.S. by Kids Can Press Ltd.
25 Dockside Drive, Toronto, ON M5A 0B5

Kids Can Press is a Corus Entertainment Inc. company
www.kidscanpress.com

The artwork in this book was rendered digitally.
The text is set in Picadilly.

Edited by Kathleen Keenan
Designed by Barb Kelly

Printed and bound in Shenzhen, China,
in 10/2022 by C & C Offset

CM 23 0 9 8 7 6 5 4 3 2 1

Library and Archives Canada Cataloguing in Publication

Title: The best way to get your way / written by Tanya Lloyd Kyi ;
illustrated by Chanelle Nibbelink.
Names: Kyi, Tanya Lloyd, 1973– author. | Nibbelink, Chanelle, illustrator.
Identifiers: Canadiana 2022022417X | ISBN 9781525305481 (hardcover)
Subjects: LCSH: Debates and debating — Juvenile literature. | LCSH: Reasoning —
Juvenile literature. | LCSH: Public speaking—Juvenile literature.
Classification: LCC PN4181 .K95 2023 | DDC j808.53 — dc23

Kids Can Press gratefully acknowledges that the land on which our office is located is the traditional territory of many nations, including the Mississaugas of the Credit, the Anishnabeg, the Chippewa, the Haudenosaunee and the Wendat peoples, and is now home to many diverse First Nations, Inuit and Métis peoples.

We thank the Government of Ontario, through Ontario Creates; the Ontario Arts Council; the Canada Council for the Arts; and the Government of Canada for supporting our publishing activity.

Contents

Introduction

MAKE YOUR BED.

Finish your **HOMEWORK.**

PUT DOWN that screen.

You've probably heard these orders before. And you're a kid. What choice do you have? How could you possibly convince your mom that she's wrong about early bedtimes? Or tell your dad to stop serving salad with dinner?

Well, you've opened the right book!

The Best Way to Get Your Way is about debate skills. A "debate" is a formal way of having an argument. It can be used in all sorts of situations.

- In court, lawyers appear in front of a judge and debate whether there's enough **evidence** to prove that someone's committed a crime.
- We watch online or on TV as politicians stand at microphones and debate about the best ways to lead the country.
- In schools and universities, debate teams meet to argue against teams from other schools.

School debate clubs tackle issues from whether phones should be allowed in classrooms to whether waffles are better than pancakes. One team takes the **affirmative**, or "yes," side, and the other team takes the **negative**, or "no," side. Then the battle begins!

In the debate between waffles and pancakes, French toast is the clear winner.

SILAS MARIA LILY AMIR BRENDAN

The Kitchen Court

Formal debates don't usually happen around the kitchen table ... until now. After reading these chapters, you'll know all the pros and cons of cleanliness, screen time, veggie servings, early bedtimes and homework. You'll be able to choose your side, use solid research to support your case, and state your views clearly. You'll even be able to handle any tricky counter-arguments your family members throw your way.

The goal of this book isn't to convince you (or your parents) that broccoli servings should be gobbled up, or that homework should be banned forever. Most debate questions don't have clear right or wrong answers. You'll have to check out the research, read the pros and cons and then choose for yourself.

You may decide that screen-time limits are reasonable. Or you might argue that you should get unlimited coding practice on weekends. Either way, you'll have the facts, the critical-thinking skills and the debate know-how needed to defend your position.

Get ready to gain some persuasion superpowers.

The Debaters

Meet our star debaters. These 10 students signed up for the school's debate club, eager to tackle big issues and controversies. They're fierce competitors who never back away from a word-wrestling match. Each will try to win your support in the upcoming chapters, so read their arguments carefully and decide who battles best.

| RILEY | IZZY | BENJIRO | HAILEY | BECCA |

CHAPTER 1

Get Your Way about Chores

A formal debate always starts with a **resolution**. That's a fancy word for a statement about a topic. Here's the topic we'll be discussing in the next few pages:

Kids should clean their rooms.

Silas will argue that tidiness is terrific. Maria disagrees. She says that sometimes, mess is magnificent.

Who will make the more convincing points? Dust off your curiosity and see what you decide …

Opening Statement: Silas
The Case for Clean

Of course we should keep our rooms tidy! The skills we learn while straightening our sheets and organizing our desks can make us more successful in life.

It's time to clear away the cobwebs and take a close look at the research behind cleanliness. Here's what the science says:

- Kids who do chores are nice and have tons of friends.
- People in clean rooms make more logical decisions.
- Mess-free is stress-free. Clean rooms help keep us calm.

Don't let the opposing side clutter your brain with illogical points. Instead, stay clearly on the side of my clean and organized arguments.

The Case for Clutter

Making your bed is a waste of time.

Do you really want to spend precious hours folding your laundry and organizing your pencils? Why not embrace a bit of chaos? It might take longer to find your socks, but you'll get lots of benefits in return:

- People in messy environments are more creative. They're willing to take risks, and they think in more imaginative ways.
- A lot of genius scientists and inventors were famous for their messy desks.
- Girls do way more chores than boys. If we *all* refuse to make our beds, we'll achieve gender equality!

It's possible we were born to be geniuses. But if we're forced to clean our rooms — and clear away our creativity — how will we ever find out?

Ruling with Research

Maria and Silas have outlined their main points. Now they need to present evidence.

Debaters often use examples from history. They might also speak about their own personal experiences. But the most convincing debate arguments always rely on scientific research. Let's see what evidence Maria and Silas use to argue the messy question of room cleaning ...

Thinking outside the Hamper

Kathleen Vohs is a professor at the University of Minnesota. She and her team of researchers assigned some students to orderly rooms with neat piles of paper. Others, they sent to cluttered rooms where the table — and the floor! — were strewn with office supplies. They gave all the students a simple task: brainstorm 10 new ways to use Ping-Pong balls.

The students in the clean rooms made suggestions that were close to the ways Ping-Pong balls are already used. Adapt the balls for slightly different games, they said.

Students in the messy rooms had more innovative ideas: cut the tops from the balls and use them as ice-cube trays, or stick them to the bottoms of chairs so the chair legs don't scratch the floor.

Kathleen and her team concluded that messy spaces help people think in new ways.

The world has lots of problems that need creative solutions. We want to become inventive, out-of-the-box thinkers. A bit of mess is obviously best.

It's a Clean Sweep

In a 2019 study, researchers at the University of Virginia asked almost 10 000 kindergartners about their chores. The scientists visited the same kids a few years later, when they were in third grade, and asked them questions about their lives. They discovered that kids who did chores

- made friends more easily,
- were happier and
- earned better math grades.

In another study, Canadian and Australian researchers asked parents and teachers to record when kids did kind, helpful things.

Imagine you were part of that study, and your mom was secretly tracking you. She might make a check mark if you took the dog for a walk without being asked. Your teacher might make a check mark if you helped your friend with his math.

Here's what the scientists found: kids who did their chores without being asked were more likely to show care and concern for other people.

So ... why make your bed? Because making your bed means you're a better person.

Rebut What?

Next up in this raging debate: the rebuttals.

Rebuttals are counterarguments.

Let's imagine your kitchen smells bad.

"The dog farted," Mom says.

"But Dad took the dog for a walk," you say.

You've presented a rebuttal by using evidence to argue against your mom's statement.* Turn the page to find out what rebuttals Silas and Maria will come up with!

* The writer of this book is in no way implying that your mom farts.

Tidy Desk, Tidy Mind

Who cares if messy desks spark creativity? Clean spaces help us make more logical decisions.

Everyone knows bed-makers grow into successful people. In a 2019 study, Kathleen Vohs showed that people in messy rooms have better Ping-Pong-ball ideas. But her team did two other experiments with clean rooms and messy rooms. In one, Dutch students were asked if they would like to donate to a charity that gives books and toys to children. The students sitting in clean rooms gave twice as much money.

Next, Kathleen asked 188 adults to review a snack-bar menu. The people in the messy spaces chose unfamiliar ingredients to add to their smoothies. (As Maria argued, messiness might make us more open to new ideas.) But the people in clean spaces were much more likely to choose healthier ingredients.

Clean, organized rooms make us nicer, more generous, healthier people. Does it really matter if we're a little less creative?

Mess Is Best

Some studies have shown that bed-making kids become more successful. But there are lots of reasons super-tidy kids might grow into influential adults. Maybe bed-making kids have more involved parents. Maybe they live in more privileged families.

Is their future success really *caused* by smoothing their sheets each morning? I think that's an example of correlation, not causation.

Besides, there are plenty of highly successful people whose desks look like pigpens:

- Albert Einstein, physics mastermind
- Barack Obama, former President of the United States
- Arianna Huffington, founder of the *Huffington Post*

Would you rather be a chores genius or a creative genius? Maybe it's time to embrace the chaos and free your mind.

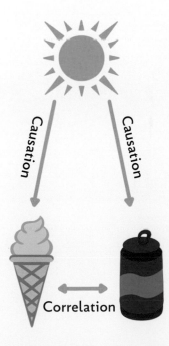

Same but Different

If you want to argue effectively, there are two big words you should know.

- **Causation** means that one thing causes another. Lightning causes thunder, and earthquakes cause tsunamis.
- **Correlation** means that two things are connected, but one doesn't necessarily produce the other.

Imagine you own a corner store. You notice that on some days, you sell more cold drinks *and* more ice-cream cones. There's a correlation. But is there causation? Of course not! Cold drink sales don't cause ice cream sales. They're both probably caused by something else ... something like hot, sunny weather outside.

No Mess, No Stress

When you try to calm yourself, what do you picture? Probably a clear, open space. Maybe an empty room, a meadow or a beach. You don't imagine a mishmash of toys, books and dirty clothes!

Chicago professor Joseph Ferrari is an expert in clutter. Working with young adults, he's shown that people with too much stuff are more likely to procrastinate, have trouble making decisions and feel less comfortably "at home" in their spaces. Other research suggests that people with cluttered bedrooms get less sleep than they should. And subjects in a 2016 experiment ate twice as many cookies in a messy kitchen as they did in a clean kitchen — something the researchers linked to the stress of being in a disorganized environment.

It all boils down to one thing: cluttered places can cause anxiety. When we clean our rooms, we feel calmer. We increase our ability to focus. Those are big bonuses in return for a few minutes of tidying.

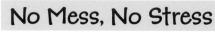

Closing Arguments: Silas

Clutter-Free Case

▸ Kids who do chores are nicer people.

▸ Clean spaces help us make more logical decisions.

▸ Organized rooms help us feel calm.

The Unfair Share

Chores are unfair to girls. According to the United Nations Children's Fund (UNICEF), girls between the ages of five and fourteen spend 40 percent more time doing housework than boys of the same age. Countries in the Middle East, North Africa and South Asia have the biggest gender gaps. But girls in Europe and North America are doing more chores, too.

Dr. Anju Malhotra is an expert in gender and health policy who has worked with the United Nations for more than a decade. She says that by doing more chores, "girls sacrifice important opportunities to learn, grow and just enjoy their childhood."

This gap should worry everyone. We want to teach all kids that they're equal, with equal responsibilities around the home. But if you're a girl, it's extra concerning. So why not take a stand by refusing to straighten your bed? You'll be making the world a more equal place.

Closing Arguments: Maria

Creative Chaos

- People in messy spaces are more creative.
- Many famous geniuses were messy.
- Chores are unfair to girls.

Decision Time

You're the judge in this debate. So whose side will you choose? You can make your room a neat and shiny space, free of distractions. Or you can try convincing your parents that a den of disorder will help you become a creative genius. When the sun rises tomorrow morning, and your parents tell you to tidy ...

Which way is your way?

CHAPTER 2

Get Your Way about Screens

Grandma says too many video games will turn you into a zombie. In her day, kids played outside. But you're at level 99 and there are only a few more chests to open ... do you really need to stop?

Here's the resolution for this chapter's debate: *Kids should have less screen time.*

Amir agrees with Grandma — TV and video games aren't healthy. On the other side of the debate, Lily will argue that gaming prepares us for a high-tech future.

Opening Statement: Amir
Let's Get Real

It's time to disconnect. When we're glued to our tablets, phones and gaming consoles, we're cheating ourselves and cheating the world.

- TV-watching kids are way less healthy. They get less exercise than other kids.
- Extra screen time is linked to anxiety, and no one needs more stress.
- If you spend all your time clicking online, you might lose the ability to "click" in real life. Less time on your devices means more in-person time with friends.

If a doctor offered you an invisible pill to make you healthier, happier and more popular, would you take it? Well, that pill exists! It's called the turn-off-your-screen pill. You can take it today.

Screen Time for the Win

We need screens like we need air. They connect, educate and entertain us. Telling a kid to stop using a phone is like telling the human race to stop using the wheel. Why take away a world-changing invention? Here are a few benefits of screen time:

- Gaming improves our fine-motor skills and helps us learn math and science.
- Screens connect us to friends, relatives and teachers all over the world.
- Doing good things online encourages us to do good in the real world.

All around the world, people are discovering the amazing things that screens can do. Why go back to the prehistoric age? Instead, let's use today's technologies to change our lives and improve the world.

The Power of Practice

If you're presenting an argument in person, practice in front of the mirror first. Or record yourself and watch the video.

See if you do these things:
- ✓ stand up straight with your shoulders back
- ✓ speak slowly and clearly
- ✓ make eye contact with the audience
- ✓ use a few subtle hand motions
- ✓ smile or nod when appropriate

Doing any of these things will help you seem clearer and more confident.

Screen Slugs

In 2019, British researchers Neza Stiglic and Russell Viner looked at studies of kids and screen time from all over the world. Here's what they found:

- More screen time = less physical activity.
- More screen time = more junk food.

Other scientists have found similar results, and it doesn't seem to make a difference what country kids live in, what ethnicity they are or how much money their families make.

You might be thinking, "I make up for screen time with lots of soccer."

Nope, it doesn't work that way.

Kids who balance their hours of TV with extra hours of sports *still* get the bad effects of screens. When you're at school, you break up your study time with physical education, walks through the hallways and trips to the playground. Our bodies need that sort of regular movement.

Forget this debate. Let's head to the skate park!

Level Up

Your favorite video game might be your first step toward medical school.

In 2016, researchers in Switzerland asked medical students to play five different video games. Then, they asked the students to perform a virtual-reality knee surgery. The students who were best at first-person shooter and 3D sports games did better on the operation. They quickly learned to use the tools, find problems within the knee joints and "hook" tiny objects.

It turns out video games help improve our hand-eye coordination and teach us to block out distractions. So next time your dad says to turn off the console, tell him you're busy ... studying for medical school.

Strong Sources

Your little brother says your Halloween candy is poisonous, and you should give it all to him so he can dispose of it safely. Do you believe him?

Of course not!
1. He's not a qualified chemist or doctor.
2. He hasn't shown you research to back up his claim.
3. He may have a **bias**. His own goals might affect his ability to make a fair judgment.

When preparing for a debate, you need to find reliable sources of information. Government websites, university websites and science journals are all good sources for debate research. Little brothers ... not so much.

Alien Ideas

You've heard aliens are attacking New York City. Where can you check to see if this is true?

Trustworthy Sources:
- The NASA website
- An astrophysicist at a major university
- The *New York Times*

Questionable Sources:
- "My Alien Encounter" blog post
- Your friend Ethan
- The Aliens 'R' Us social media page

Screens Aren't Created Equal

Too much sitting isn't great for our bodies. We can all agree on that. But sitting and gaming are two different things.

Gaming requires different postures than TV watching. When we're racing around a virtual track or hunting an enemy sniper, we sit up straight and tense our core muscles. We might even dodge and weave as our characters move on-screen.

And some video games are created to keep us moving. These Active Video Games, or AVGs, use sensors to track player movements and copy them on-screen. During the beginning of the COVID-19 pandemic, Cristina Comeras-Chueca and her fellow researchers at the University of Zaragoza in Spain investigated these AVGs. They found that after kids played regularly for a few months, their fitness levels and motor skills increased. A 2021 Brazilian study found the games helped with mental health, too.

So next time you're sitting down, play a video game!

Screen-Free Fun

Most video games *aren't* exercise. And plenty of experts say kids should be running around outside, screen-free.

In 2020, American researcher Jennifer Zink examined 46 different studies from around the world. She found a link between video-game playing and depression, and the link was stronger for boys and for young people who weren't physically active.

Even famous technology executives — people who have made millions of dollars selling devices and games — control their kids' screen time. Bill Gates, the founder of Microsoft, put strict limits on his daughter's gaming. Steve Jobs, the man who made iPhones and iPads famous, didn't let his own kids use the devices.

People who actually invent tech realize that screens can be addictive and unhealthy.

Guess what helps protect *against* depression? Time in nature! Let's put our screens away, grab our bikes and head for the nearest green space.

Authority Figures

A **fallacy** is an illogical argument. It's an error in reasoning.

Debaters label fallacies with fancy Latin terms, like *argumentum ad verecundiam*. That's a false argument that relies on an authority figure. Have you ever seen ads like this?

"Six out of seven dentists agree that space travel is wonderful."

"Basketball star Danny McDribble loves our new hair gel!"

Dentists are trusted health professionals, so people tend to believe them. We also believe doctors, nurses, lab-coat-wearing scientists ... and famous athletes.

But dentists aren't experts in space travel, and athletes aren't experts in hair gel. Using their authority-figure status to advertise unrelated things doesn't make sense. If we stop to think, we quickly spot the fallacy.

Axe the Antisocial Screens

Run around with a virtual gun and virtually shoot at virtual people? No thanks!

In 2020, the American Psychological Association wrote that violent video games made kids less empathetic and sometimes led to aggressive behavior — insults, threats, hitting, pushing and hair-pulling. In other words, if you play hours of violent video games, you might not be as nice to other people afterward.

When we go screen-free, we can focus on connecting with others. In 2014, researchers in California tested sixth-graders after a screen-free summer camp. Those kids were better at reading facial expressions than other kids who'd spent the week in school and on their screens.

Reading subtle social cues can help you be a great friend. You'll know when your besties are sad, when they're mad and when they're happy. So sacrifice some screen time and become a BFF.

Closing Arguments: Amir

Anti-Tech Talk

▸ Screen time makes kids less healthy.

▸ Too many video games can lead to anxiety and depression.

▸ Screens make us antisocial. We need to spend more time with real-life friends.

Save Our Screens!

I use my phone to keep in touch with my grandparents. And my computer lets me take online classes or learn about things I've never seen in real life. (Did you know there are miniature African antelopes called dik-diks that look like bouncy baby deer?)

Amir says screens make us antisocial. But playing cooperative games can actually make people more helpful. In 2018, researchers in Utah reviewed 72 studies about **prosocial** behavior — people helping other people. The studies examined this type of behavior on TV shows, in video games, in songs, in books and on websites. They found prosocial media made kids more helpful, more empathetic and less aggressive.

So don't ditch the screens altogether! If you're worried about violence and video games, play cooperative games instead. Or research miniature antelopes.

Closing Arguments: Lily

Dream Screens

▸ Gaming increases our hand-eye coordination.

▸ Active video games are good for our fitness and our mental health.

▸ Cooperative video games can make us more helpful people and connect us with others around the world.

Decision Time

No one understands exactly how screens affect our brains and bodies. Scientists have ideas, and they have research that's starting to point in one direction or the other. But there are no golden rules for how much screen time is best or which video games might warp your mind.

You've read Amir's arguments for skipping your screen time and Lily's points in favor of saving it. Now it's time to decide ...

Which way is your way?

CHAPTER 3

Get Your Way about Vegetables

Health experts say fruits and veggies should take up half our plates. At EVERY MEAL. What?! Are they really that important?

Here's the resolution for this chapter's debate:
Kids should eat more vegetables.

Brendan is gaga for green. He loves lettuce, adores asparagus and sings serenades to spinach each evening. He'll be arguing the affirmative — that vegetables are vital.

Riley says greens make them gag. They'll take the negative, arguing we should trash our turnips and chuck our chard.

Crunch on these arguments and decide what you believe ...

Opening Statement: Brendan
Rock the Broc!

When experts tell us to wear our seat belts, we buckle up. When experts tell us to protect our skin, we slap on sunscreen. But when experts tell us to eat more greens, we ... order more hamburgers instead.

That's right, health organizations in Canada and the United States say kids are eating fewer vegetables than ever before. What's going on?

There are a lot of advantages to eating green:

• Parents are right — veggies are good for us.

  • A plant-based diet is better for the planet.

  • People who eat plants are happier.

We're not toddlers anymore. It's time to put on our big-kid pants and crunch those carrots.

Veggie Rebellion

Why are we still worrying about vegetables? There are A LOT of good foods in the world. We could choose a different dish each day and never run out of new things to try. So it's time to eat the things we like and relax about the broccoli. Here's why:

- Our bodies can get vitamins and minerals in all sorts of non-vegetable ways.
- Forcing kids to eat vegetables causes stress for the whole family — and it doesn't work.
- Kids learn their eating habits from their parents, so maybe parents should check their own fruit and vegetable intake and leave ours alone.

Do I think vegetables are good for you? Sure. But are there other options? Of course! So, if you'll excuse me, I have to go and finish a perfectly nutritious plate of bacon.

Veggie Overload

Eat your vegetables. Eat your vegetables! *Eat your vegetables!!*

Yeesh ... enough already.

We all know salad is nutritious. But to some people — like me — lettuce tastes like lawn mower clippings. And there are plenty of other places we can find our vitamins and minerals. Apricots are rich in vitamin A, bananas are bursting with potassium and oranges pack a vitamin C punch.

Even fruits are optional. Some cultures have always eaten diets high in meat and fat, with few greens. The traditional Inuit diet consists of meats such as seal, caribou and whale. The Sámi, Indigenous peoples of northern Scandinavia, traditionally relied on fish and reindeer meat. People lived well that way for thousands of years, and some still do.

I'm not suggesting a reindeer-only diet works for everyone. But vitamins and minerals exist in all sorts of foods. We shouldn't be forced to eat squash.

Global Greens

When you choose what to eat for breakfast, do you survey all the foods in the whole world, then decide? Of course not. Your choices depend on where you live, what religion you follow, how much money your family can spend on groceries and a whole list of other factors. All of these things affect how many vegetables you eat, too.

Which breakfast do you like best?

Embrace the Endive

Scientists know that fruits and vegetables reduce our risk of high blood pressure, heart disease, stroke and obesity. Researchers think they probably help reduce our risk of cancer and diabetes. And veggies might even help prevent eye disease, dementia and asthma. But what's actually happening inside our bodies?

Ha-Nul Lee and a team of researchers in South Korea decided to find out. For their 2021 study, they took samples of bone marrow tissue. (It produces many of our disease-fighting cells.) Next, they combined a vegetable soup extract with a nutrient supplement. Then they added a tiny bit of the veggie mix to the bone marrow tissue.

It turns out that Grandma was right all along: vegetable soup is good for you. The bone marrow tissue started pumping out extra disease-fighting cells.

So stock up on veg. You'll keep your immune system ready for action!

Lichen for Lunch, Anyone?

Riley says they can live without vegetables because Inuit eat a ton of protein and the Sámi exist on reindeer. But that's not the whole story. Traditional northern diets include berries, lichens, ocean plants and mushrooms.

Riley was right about one thing: traditional diets can teach us a lot. About balance. We have to balance our wants with the needs of our environment.

Right now, the world's meat consumption is skyrocketing. People in the United States eat an average of 26 kg (57 lb.) of beef per year. That's 228 hamburgers each!

Raising cows for beef requires huge amounts of grain and large expanses of land. Plus, cows produce methane, a greenhouse gas that contributes to global warming. So eating vegetables is better for the planet.

Eat a carrot. Save the world!

Fact Check

In some debates, teams are allowed to use a tablet or laptop to fact-check the other team's arguments. In real life, fact-checking often happens later. The morning after a political debate, for example, you'll see headlines like this:

- "Fact Check: Pauline Politician's Claims about Corn"
- "Examining Claims from Alex Antiveg"
- "The Real Truth about the Debaters' Dessert-Eating Addictions!"

Does fact-checking someone's statements really matter, when everyone's already heard the false information? It won't change everyone's mind, obviously. But studies show that when people are alerted to possible mistakes and given background information, they do stop to think more carefully.

Lester's Left Behind

Health is about choosing a variety of foods, giving yourself energy and listening to your body's signals. My tongue says it doesn't want broccoli.

Imagine this classic scene: A family has finished dinner. They're eating dessert in front of the TV. But poor Lester is still sitting at the table, alone, staring at his brussels sprouts. He's not allowed to leave until he eats them.

Is Lester learning to love vegetables? No! He's learning to ignore his own body's signals and to think of dessert as a reward and vegetables as a punishment.

At Pennsylvania State University, researchers gave vegetable soup to two groups of preschoolers. In one group, the kids were allowed to eat whatever amount they wanted. In the other group, a researcher repeated this line four times: "Eat your soup, please."

The second group didn't like being told what to do. They said things like, "Yuck, I don't like it. I don't want to eat it." But did they at least finish their soup?

No! Telling the kids to eat more had absolutely no effect.

There are already a lot of things worth stressing about. Vegetables aren't one of them.

Green Genes

Don't like veggies? Blame your parents.

Somewhere on that spiral staircase of **DNA** inside your cells, you might have genes that make you more sensitive to bitter, sweet or spicy foods. Greens might make you gag. Chilies might set your tongue on FIRE!

Even when our veggie eating isn't affected by our genes, it can be influenced by our parents' likes and dislikes. Studies in Romania and Poland found that when parents didn't like certain vegetables, they didn't buy them and didn't offer them to their kids. If your mom doesn't like cauliflower, you might never have tried it. Parents were also more likely to give their kids fruits instead of vegetables because they figured their kids would like them better.

We're not always in charge of what we eat. Your parents can nag about veggies all they want — but if they want you to change, they should adjust their own habits first!

Closing Arguments: Riley

Anti-Spinach Stance

- We can get our nutrients in other ways.
- Forcing kids to eat vegetables makes mealtimes moody.
- We learn by example, and parents don't eat their veggies either.

Cool as a Cucumber

Bananas make me happy. And not just because they have a-peel. (Get it?)

In fact, bananas are just one on a list of fruits and vegetables scientifically proven to boost our mental health. In 2018, Kate Brookie and a team of scientists in New Zealand assessed the diets of 422 young people. They tracked 10 raw foods, including carrots, apples, leafy greens, berries and cucumber. Those who ate more raw fruits and vegetables seemed happier. They reported less anxiety. They didn't suffer from depression as often. And they felt more positively about their lives.

Scientists think that in order to function well, our brains need the vitamins and minerals that raw veggies provide. So next time you're feeling tired and sluggish, maybe it's time to start crunching!

Closing Arguments: Brendan

Crush on Cauliflower

▸ Vegetables make us healthier.

▸ Eating plants instead of meat is better for the planet.

▸ Eating vegetables helps our mental health and overall mood.

Decision Time

Brendan has made a convincing case. Veggies are obviously good for us. But Riley has some good points, too. If you really hate veggies, are they worth the trauma?

In real life, we often **compromise**. We meet our debate opponent (um ... parent) halfway. But that's not the case here. In a formal debate, we have to choose which side is most convincing ...

Which way is your way?

CHAPTER 4

Get Your Way about Bedtime

The clock tick-tocks toward bedtime. Do you yawn and say goodnight? Or do you cling to the TV remote, hug the couch cushions and refuse to leave the living room?

Here's the resolution for this chapter:

Kids should go to bed early.

Izzy believes we need our sleep to keep us healthy and happy. But Benjiro says bedtime was invented to torture kids and make them miss life's most exciting moments. He says we should sacrifice sleep — at least sometimes — in exchange for more fun.

Whose arguments are doze-worthy, and whose will wake your interest? Read on (as long as it's not past your bedtime) and see what you decide.

Opening Statement: Izzy
Sweet Dreams

A fluffy pillow, a cozy duvet, a reading lamp and a great book ... why would anyone want to avoid bedtime? Life is fun, but it's also busy, overwhelming and sometimes stressful. Thank goodness we can tuck ourselves in and forget our troubles.

There are plenty of good, scientific reasons why we need our shut-eye:

- Sleep is when our bodies do most of their healing and growing.
- The learning we do during the day is sorted and stored by our brains at night.
- After a few extra hours of rest, we're faster and more coordinated.

We all stay up late occasionally. But "occasionally" should be the key word. Most nights, we should turn down the lights and drift happily into dreamland.

Opening Statement: Benjiro
The Wake-Up Shake-Up

SO MANY COOL THINGS happen after 9 p.m. There are sleepovers and movie nights, school dances and fireworks displays, stargazing parties and campouts with s'mores. Who has time to sleep?

Wake up to your new, active life with these anti-sleep arguments:

- Bedtime is cultural. In different parts of the world, kids go to bed at vastly different times.
- Experiences like summer camp and sleepovers are worth losing rest.
- Scientists say grown-ups can't catch up on lost sleep — but kids can.

Of course we need to sleep sometimes. But open your eyes. Smell the late-night popcorn! We don't always need to hit the pillow right before the fun begins.

Bedtimes and Borders

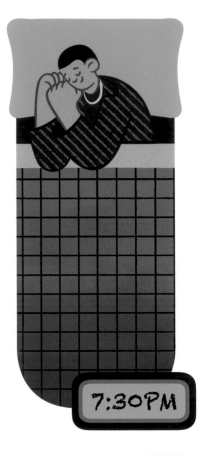

You are entering the City of New York. Please be advised: bedtime is 8 p.m.

Have you ever seen a road sign like that? Of course not! Because bedtime isn't a law. It's a rule made up by your parents. And in different parts of the world, parents have different rules.

In the Netherlands, parents tuck kids into their beds at about 7:30 p.m. But in Spain, even toddlers stay up until 10 p.m. or later. They catch up on dream-time during afternoon siestas. And in other countries, such as many in South America, kids fall asleep around the same time as their parents and take daytime catnaps if they need to.

So next time your dad says it's time to hit the pillow, tell him bedtime is a cultural construct. Then ask if your family can move to Spain.

Doze Data

As you hit puberty, getting to sleep on time gets trickier. That's because of something called "phase delay." The hormonal changes happening in teens' bodies make it harder to go to sleep early ... and *much* harder to wake up in the morning.

Scientists know all this because of a sleep researcher named Mary Carskadon, who has somehow convinced hundreds of teens to go to "summer camp" in an underground bunker, where she studies their sleep habits.

Before you decide that Mary's work sounds a bit extreme, consider this: she's convinced high schools around the world to start their classes later so kids can keep snoozing!

Brain Drain

On the street, talking to a lamppost. That's where 17-year-old student Randy Gardner found himself after staying awake for four days as part of a science-fair project. This is a terrible and dangerous idea for a project, but Randy went to high school in the 1960s. Back then, people didn't yet understand the value of sleep.

Our bodies need to snooze! During those hours of shut-eye, our immune systems work overtime. Sleep helps stabilize our heart rates, our hormones and our digestion. While we rest, our cells repair damage to our DNA, healing us on a microscopic level.

Plus, you know how some animals, like skunks and hedgehogs, are nocturnal, meaning active at night? So are our growth hormones! If you're hoping to grow taller or stronger, a good night's sleep is your best bet.

Science-fair goofball Randy Gardner stayed awake for a total of nine days. He wound up paranoid, confused and unable to count backward from 100. Don't be like Randy. Get to bed on time. And instead of lampposts, talk to the weird creatures in your dreams.

Rebuttal: Benjiro
What a Snore

Izzy, no offense, but your arguments are a nightmare. If you want to do everything your parents tell you to do, from A to Zzzzzz, you go right ahead. The rest of us would rather stay up and have fun.

Ever heard of fireworks displays before 8 p.m.? Nope. How many meteor showers do you get to watch if you're tucked into bed before dark? None. And don't even think about going to a school dance.

Maybe you've never seen fireworks, shooting stars or my amazing dance moves because you're already in dreamland. Maybe you don't know what you're missing. That's fine. Keep snoozing your life away. The rest of us are going out!

Latin for Losers

Don't listen to him! He's a liar!

In fancy Latin lingo, that's called an *argumentum ad hominem*, an "argument against the person." It's an argument in which someone attacks the speaker's character, usually to distract listeners from the facts.

You might have seen a debate like this on the news:

Politician A: We need to build an awesome new school.

Politician B: Who says "awesome" anymore? He's so old. And his hair looks funny.

The second politician is hoping listeners will be so busy considering hairstyles and wrinkles that they'll forget about the school altogether.

Lights Out

You'll have to excuse my opponent, Benjiro. He's obviously lacking sleep.

You see, scientists have proved that without sleep we don't learn as well, we have trouble remembering things and we can't reason as well. That's probably why Benjiro's arguments are so ridiculous.

Italian sleep scientists Chiara Cirelli and Giulio Tononi have a theory about sleep and our brains. During the day, as we learn new things, our nerve cells burn a lot of energy. They're growing new connections and adapting to our needs. But they also get tired. During the night, when it's dark and quiet, those nerve cells get a rest. The most important connections from your day (those multiplication tables you learned, for example) are strengthened. The less important ones (the fact that your trash can smells) are whisked away. In the morning, your brain is tidied up and ready to learn again.

Even one late night can cause troubles with attention and memory. Plus, studies show sleep-deprived people can't appreciate humor as well. This explains my opponent's terrible puns. He needs a good night's sleep.

It's Party Time

Congratulations! You're invited to sleep-away camp. You'll play flashlight tag in the woods, roast s'mores and sing campfire songs late into the night.

Wait ... you can't go? Because you need nine and a half hours of sleep a night?

Don't be ridiculous. Some things are worth a little sleep loss.

And scientists say that while adults can't catch up on lost sleep, kids can! One study by the National Sleep Foundation found that kids who sleep seven hours a night, instead of the recommended nine and a half, were at higher risk for weight gain. But the risk was lower for kids who caught up with weekend sleep-ins.

Sometimes life is too exciting to snooze through. So relax about bedtime, have some fun and catch up on Sunday morning. You'll have great summer-camp memories forever.

Closing Arguments: Benjiro

Wide-Eyed Ways

- Bedtimes aren't laws, just rules made up by our parents.
- Some experiences — like summer camp — are better than sleep.
- Party now, and catch up on sleep later.

Fitter and Faster

What do you need to play in the NBA? Some hoop skills. Check. A great jump shot. Check. Height and strength. Check.

And ... great sleep habits.

What?

Professional athletes jet across time zones, play far into the night and get up early for practice. But over the last decade, many have realized that sleep is vital to playing their best. Sports teams have even hired sleep coaches. Charles Czeisler is a senior physician at Harvard. He's worked with teams around the world, and he tells them sleep is critical. Before the game, extra rest helps with coordination and quick thinking. After the game, it helps players remember new skills.

My opponent, Benjiro, loves to play basketball. If he'd like to improve his game, I'd suggest he skip the sleepover and focus on more sleep instead.

Closing Arguments: Izzy

Dreamy Debate Points

▸ Sleep keeps us healthy and helps us grow.

▸ People who sleep more are smarter.

▸ Sleep makes us faster and more coordinated.

Decision Time

Who won the great wake debate?

Both debaters took some time away from presenting evidence to personally attack their opponent. In the midst of an argument, it can be hard to focus on logic. But to judge a debate fairly, we need to weigh facts, not emotional outbursts. So ask yourself: did the debaters clearly explain their positions, using evidence to back up their cases?

Oh, your mom's calling. She says to turn out your light.

Which way is your way?

CHAPTER 5

Get Your Way about Homework

Your math problems seem to stretch into eternity. Your reading assignments are piled so high they teeter above your head. Do you really have to do all this work?

Hailey and Becca are ready to tackle homework head-on, debating the following resolution:

Kids should do their homework.

Becca will argue that homework teaches kids good study skills and turns them into responsible human beings. Hailey says homework stresses out students and parents, and those math worksheets should go straight to the recycling bin.

Who will win the schoolwork spat? Study hard (or not), and see what you decide.

Opening Statement: Becca
Sharpen Your Pencils

You can whine about your homework, or you can sit down and finish it. If you ace your essays and polish your projects, you'll reap the rewards: improved grades and organizational skills. So get to work!

- Homework helps us become responsible, organized people.
- Homework doesn't have to be boring. When kids are given choices, they're more motivated to study.
- Homework shows us that brainpower isn't only for the classroom. We can learn new things anywhere.

Let's make peace with our papers and pens.

Save Our Students!

Just because we're not doing homework doesn't mean we're not learning. Jamming in the garage, playing pick-up soccer or competing in your family board game tournament ... these are all valuable activities. Life is about more than math.

Let's erase the tradition of doing extra schoolwork after school.

- Studies show that homework has no learning benefits for kids in elementary school.
- Too much homework creates stress for students and their parents.
- Kids need time to hang out with friends, make mac and cheese and draw manga characters. They need life skills just as much as science skills maybe more.

It's time for teachers to rid themselves of reading lists. School swallows up more than six hours a day. Leave us alone for the few hours that remain.

Space Race

In the early 1900s, homework was considered bad for kids' health. The *Ladies' Home Journal* magazine declared kids should be playing outside and getting extra sleep instead of studying. Homework was even declared illegal in California.

But when Russia was first to send a satellite into space in 1957, Americans worried that their society was falling behind. The answer? More homework for everyone. Today, American students do an average of about one and a half hours per day.

Dr. Homework

Harris Cooper is a homework expert. More officially, he's an education researcher at Duke University in North Carolina. And he's reviewed almost every American homework experiment ever created. Here are some of the things he's found:

- High school students can handle about two hours a night. After that, their brains become overloaded and they start forgetting things.
- Junior high students can do about an hour a night.
- Homework in elementary school has no benefits to learning. None!

Other scientists have shown that a bit of studying — even in elementary school — helps with math and science skills. But those subjects are the exception.

So next time your sixth-grade French teacher tries to send home a worksheet, try explaining (in French, of course) that homework won't do your brain a bit of good. *Mais non, merci!*

Practice Makes Perfect

"Conscientiousness." That's the word researchers use for a group of personality traits including responsibility, reliability and dedication. Conscientious people show up to their competitive hopscotch tournaments on time, get their chores done and return their library books by the due date.

All of these responsible habits pay off. Conscientious kids are more likely to have good friends and successful careers once they grow up.

So how can we become more like them? Well, German scientist Richard Göllner came up with one interesting answer: homework. For his 2017 study, he recruited 2760 students in grades five through eight. The ones who put extra effort into their homework were more responsible, organized and contented people.

But wait ... maybe everyone becomes more organized in middle school? Nope. The researchers also tested kids who didn't try harder on homework. Those kids showed no increase in conscientiousness.

So crack open your textbook and find contentment!

Homework in Finnish Is Kotitehtäviä

Every year, Finnish kids ace achievement tests.

Experts want to know why. It's not extra homework. Finland has one of the lowest homework rates, at 2.8 hours per week. And it's not extra hours. Kids don't even attend school until they're seven years old.

But Finland values something called "comprehensive education," which means learning is free and everyone goes to similar schools, whatever their gender, religion or income. And teaching is a highly respected job that requires a master's degree.

Could those be the reasons Finnish kids are doing so well? Maybe. The experts are still doing their homework, trying to figure it out!

Homework Headaches

You don't want to do your science-fair project. It seems overwhelming. You can't sleep at night, worrying about it.

Your parents really, really want you to do your science-fair project. They say you're being irresponsible and disrespectful to your teacher.

So what happens? Stress! You avoid looking at your mom's disappointed face and you sleep even less than you did before. Even your goldfish seems to be scowling. Becca says that homework helps us become responsible people, but how can that happen when we're too stressed to think straight?

Even parents don't like homework! In a 2015 study of 2000 parents, two-thirds said they couldn't help with their kids' homework — because it was too hard. About half said they used Google to find the answers when their kids weren't looking!

Everyone in my class agrees. Our parents need to relax, we need to focus on time with our friends and — most importantly — our schoolwork needs to stay at school.

Time Management

Hailey mentioned science fair. That's an important thing to think about. Life is busy with track practices and movie nights, debate club and babysitting gigs. It's not going to get less busy as we get older. We need to learn now how to balance our time.

Besides, homework doesn't have to be a boring chore. What if we could choose our assignments, the same way we choose our hobbies? Erika Patall is an education and psychology professor at the University of Southern California. When she was a Ph.D. student, she created an experiment to study homework and choice. She and her colleagues gave assignments to about 200 high school students. Half of the students were stuck with specific assignments. But the half who were allowed to choose between two options were more motivated and earned better grades.

We don't need less homework. We simply need to be treated like responsible human beings. We should have choices for our after-school hours.

Repeat

Did not. Did too! Did not. Did too! Did not. Did too!

Ever have an argument like that one? Well, debaters tend to use words that are a bit more sophisticated. But they do love repetition. Here's why:

- Repetition helps people remember key ideas.
- Repetition creates drama and emphasis.
- Repetition can make things seem true.

When you're preparing an argument, decide on your key points. Then find ways to state, clarify and echo those points for the most dramatic impact. Repeat!*

* Give this a try with your friends. Several times a day for the next week, explain how amazing you are. On Friday, see if any of them agree.

Learning for Life

We're not going to spend our whole lives cooped up in classrooms, scribbling in our notebooks. Eventually, we're going to graduate to the real world, with all of its puzzles and problems. We're going to need to make plans, organize our supplies and finish our projects — all without a teacher leaning over our shoulders.

Homework teaches us to work hard and embrace challenges outside the classroom. By completing our assignments, we prove to ourselves we can get things done. And by taking responsibility for our own work, we become independent learners.

When we leave our desks behind, do our brains stop working? Of course not! A little homework helps us carry our curiosity into the real world.

Closing Arguments: Becca

Pencil Pushing

- Homework helps us become responsible people.
- By giving choices, teachers can make homework more motivating.
- Homework helps us become lifelong learners.

Beyond the Page

I agree with Becca. All of life is about learning.

That's why we need to leave schoolwork at school and embrace the other opportunities around us. Some cities in Japan have abandoned after-school studies. Instead, students stay after class to help mop the floors and clean the classrooms, learning life skills along the way.

In 2019, an Irish school canceled homework and assigned acts of kindness instead. Each day, students were asked to connect with an elder or help out around the house, then write about their experiences in kindness diaries.

There are so many ways we can become mature, responsible, well-rounded people. Why are we stuck doing math worksheets when we could be changing the world with kindness? (Okay, maybe doing some mopping, too.)

Closing Arguments: Hailey

Study-Free Zone

- In elementary school, homework doesn't help with learning.
- Homework creates stress for families.
- Kids need life skills, not just academic skills.

Decision Time

Who gets the top grades in this homework battle?

When we debate, we often think in terms of win or lose. But not all issues have a right answer and a wrong answer. Homework is different for different students. Some whip up an essay in 20 minutes. Others struggle.

Are there different study solutions for different kids? Could there be more room for choice, as Becca suggested? If you were designing the perfect school, what would you suggest? And next time your teacher hands out science worksheets due on Friday ...

Which way is your way?

Why Debate?

What if your friends start agreeing with all your suggestions?

"Let's go skateboarding!"

"Great idea," they say.

"Don't worry about those construction signs. They're for decoration."

"You're right," they say.

"And holes are imaginary."

"Absolutely," they say.

You can probably see where this is going!

While you're at the bottom of that hole, take a moment to think about the thousands — maybe even millions — of facts and opinions floating around in your brain. Most of those facts are probably true. But a few of them are false.

So name one thing you're wrong about.

Well, that's the problem, isn't it? We don't know which of our opinions are skewed.

Kathryn Schulz is an American journalist who wrote a book about being wrong. She says that because we don't know which things we're wrong about, we go through life assuming we're right about everything. Then, when we meet someone who disagrees with us, we assume they must be mistaken.

And if we're always entirely right, and they are always entirely wrong ... we're not going to work well together.

Debate changes all of that. As debaters, we try our hardest to argue our side. But we also listen to the research and experience behind the other side's case. At the end, we might acknowledge that there were valid arguments on both sides. We might have learned something new. Maybe, we've even realized we made an error in our thinking. If we take the time to debate, to exchange ideas and — most importantly — to listen, we might just expand our minds.

Making It Official

Heading to your first formal debate?

You'll probably see a schedule that looks something like this.

Affirmative Side	Negative Side
First Speaker	First Speaker
Second Speaker	Second Speaker
Rebuttal Speaker	Rebuttal Speaker

There are all sorts of debate formats.

- You can argue as part of a team or tackle an opponent one-on-one.
- You can prepare in advance or sign up for a surprise topic. In some competitions, debaters answer questions from the other team and even from the audience.

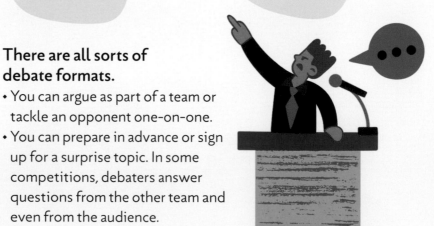

The Judges' Table

If you're in a formal debate, you'll need to impress the judges. They're looking for three things.

1
Great Content
Did you have scientific evidence? Did you use strong, trustworthy sources?

2
Speaking Style
Were you clear and confident?

3
Strategy
Did you organize your points well? How did you respond to the other side's arguments?

Quick Questions

You can probably think of a hundred topics to debate.

Here are a few to get you started:

- Should phones be allowed in classrooms?
- What's the best pizza topping: pepperoni or pineapple?
- Are report cards useful?
- Should kids get an allowance?
- Should kids wear uniforms to school?
- Should we ban junk food?
- Should all kids play sports?
- Could robots replace teachers?
- Should summer vacation be longer?
- Do aliens exist?
- Is it better to live in the city or the country?
- Should we ban plastic bags?
- Should every weekend be a three-day weekend?
- Should public transit be free for kids?
- Do princess stories promote stereotypes?

Glossary

affirmative: the team arguing in favor of the debate topic, or resolution. It can also be called the "pro" side.

bias: a pre-existing leaning toward one side of an argument or issue

causation: a connection between two things that exists because one thing causes the other

closing argument: a team's final debate speech, summarizing the evidence

compromise: an agreement in which each side gives up something, to meet in the middle

correlation: any connection between two things

DNA: a molecule inside our cells that carries our genetic code and determines many of our traits

evidence: research and facts that support an argument

fallacy: an argument that uses faulty logic

negative: the team arguing against the debate topic, or resolution. It can also be called the "con" side.

opening statement: a speech introducing the issue and summarizing the arguments to be presented

prosocial: behavior that benefits other people or society

rebuttal: an argument against the claims of the opposing team

resolution: a statement to be debated. It can also be called a topic.

Selected Sources

Brookie, Kate L., et al. "Intake of Raw Fruits and Vegetables Is Associated with Better Mental Health Than Intake of Processed Fruits and Vegetables." *Frontiers in Psychology* 9 (April 2018): 487.

Cirelli, Chiara, and Giulio Tononi. "The Sleeping Brain." *Cerebrum* (May 1, 2017): cer-07-17.

Comeras-Chueca, Cristina, et al. "The Effects of Active Video Games on Health-Related Physical Fitness and Motor Competence in Children and Adolescents with Healthy Weight: A Systematic Review and Meta-Analysis." *International Journal of Environmental Research and Public Health* 18 no. 13 (June 2021): 6965.

Coyne, Sarah M., et al. "A Meta-Analysis of Prosocial Media on Prosocial Behavior, Aggression, and Empathetic Concern : A Multidimensional Approach." *Developmental Psychology* 54, no. 2 (February 2018): 331–47.

Ferrari, Joseph R., et al. "Procrastinators and Clutter: An Ecological View of Living with Excessive "Stuff"." *Current Psychology* 37 (2018): 441–44.

Göllner, Richard, et al. "Is Doing Your Homework Associated with Becoming More Conscientious?" *Journal of Research in Personality* 71 (December 2017): 1–12.

Jentzsch, Thorsten, et al. "Correlation Between Arthroscopy Simulator and Video Game Performance : A Cross-Sectional Study of 30 Volunteers Comparing 2- and 3-Dimensional Video Games." *Arthroscopy* 32, no. 7 (July 2016): 1328–34.

Lee, Ha-Nul, et al. "Combination of Vegetable Soup and Glucan Demonstrates Synergistic Effects on Macrophage-Mediated Immune Responses." *Food Science and Biotechnology* 30, no. 4 (April 2021): 583–88.

O'Connor, Rachael. "Irish School Replaces Homework with Acts of Kindness: 'Be the Reason Somebody Smiles Today.'" *The Irish Post*, December 4, 2019.

Stiglic, Neza and Russell M. Viner. "Effects of Screentime on the Health and Well-Being of Children and Adolescents." *BMJ Open* 9, no. 1 (January 2019): e023191.

Uhls, Yalda T., et al. "Five Days at Outdoor Education Camp without Screens Improves Preteen Skills with Nonverbal Emotion Cues." *Computers in Human Behavior* 39 (October 2014): 387–92.

Vohs, Kathleen D., Joseph P. Redden, and Ryan Rahinel. "Physical Order Produces Healthy Choices, Generosity, and Conventionality, Whereas Disorder Produces Creativity." *Psychological Science* 24, no. 9 (August 1, 2013): 1860–67.

White, Elizabeth M., Mark D. DeBoer, and Rebecca J. Scharf. "Associations Between Household Chores and Childhood Self-Competency." *Journal of Developmental and Behavioral Pediatrics* 40, no. 3 (April 2019): 176–82.

Zink, Jennifer, et al. "The Relationship Between Screen-Based Sedentary Behaviors and Symptoms of Depression and Anxiety in Youth: A Systematic Review of Moderating Variables." *BMC Public Health* 20 (2020): 472.

Further Reading

Brown, Robin Terry. *Breaking the News: What's Real, What's Not, and Why the Difference Matters*. Washington, D.C.: National Geographic, 2020.

Dell, Pamela. *Understanding the News*. North Mankato, MN: Capstone Press, 2019.

Grant, John. *Debunk It!: How to Stay Sane in World of Misinformation*. San Francisco: Zest Books, 2014.

Grant, Joyce and Kathleen Marcotte. *Can You Believe It?: How to Spot Fake News and Find the Facts*. Toronto: Kids Can Press, 2022.

Paquette, Ammi-Joan, and Laurie Ann Thompson. *Two Truths and a Lie: Forces of Nature*. New York: Walden Pond Press, 2019.

Swanson, Diane, and Francis Blake. *Nibbling on Einstein's Brain: The Good, the Bad & the Bogus in Science*. Toronto: Annick Press, 2009.

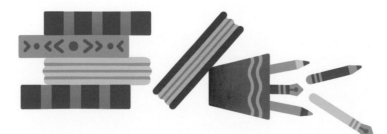

Index